SCHIRMER'S LIBRARY
OF MUSICAL CLASSICS

Vol. 2124

The Indispensable
BACH
Collection

23 Famous Piano Pieces

ISBN 978-1-4950-7158-4

G. SCHIRMER, Inc.

DISTRIBUTED BY

HAL•LEONARD®

7777 W. BLUEMOUND RD. P.O. BOX 13819 MILWAUKEE, WI 53213

www.musicsalesclassical.com
www.halleonard.com

CONTENTS

Aria da capo

from *Goldberg Variations*

Johann Sebastian Bach
BWV 988

Invention No. 1
in C Major

Johann Sebastian Bach
BWV 772

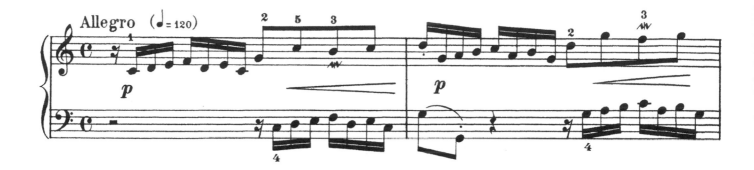

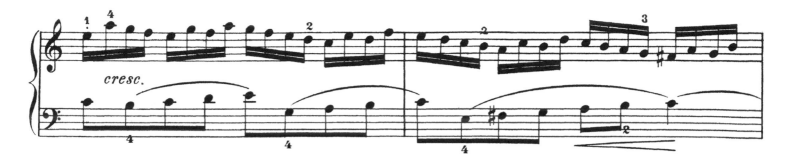

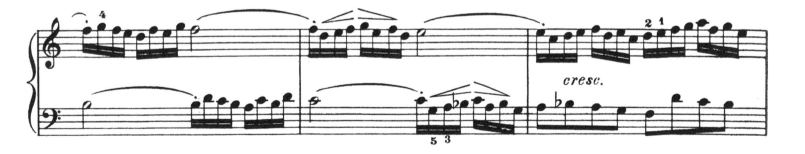

Invention No. 2
in C minor

Johann Sebastian Bach
BWV 773

Allegro moderato (♩=108)

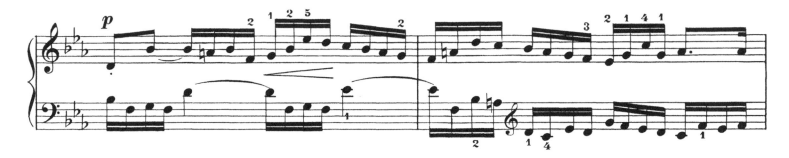

Invention No. 4
in D minor

Johann Sebastian Bach
BWV 775

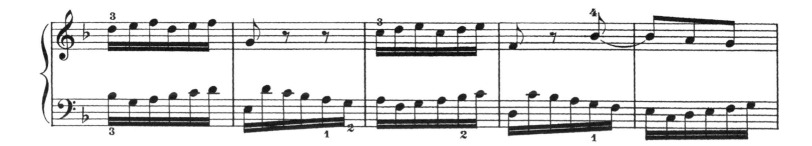

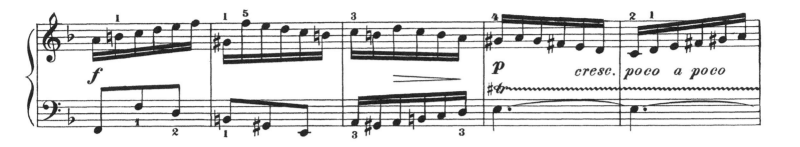

Invention No. 8
in F Major

Johann Sebastian Bach
BWV 779

Invention No. 13

in A minor

Johann Sebastian Bach
BWV 784

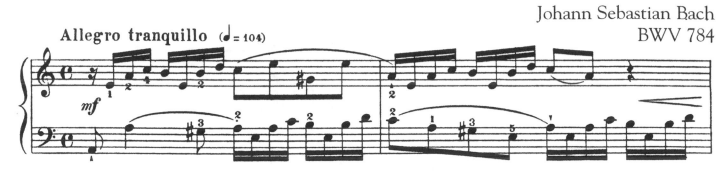

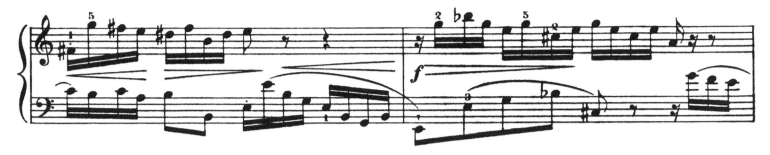

Gigue
from English Suite No. 5 in E minor

Johann Sebastian Bach
BWV 810

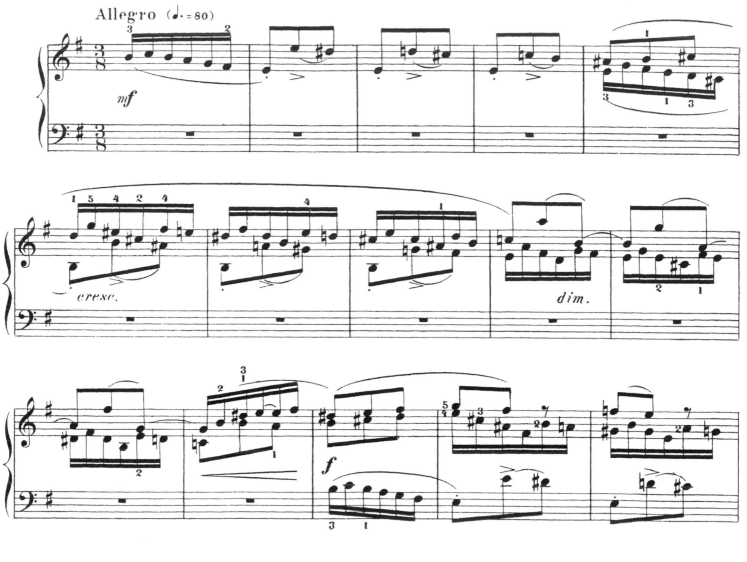

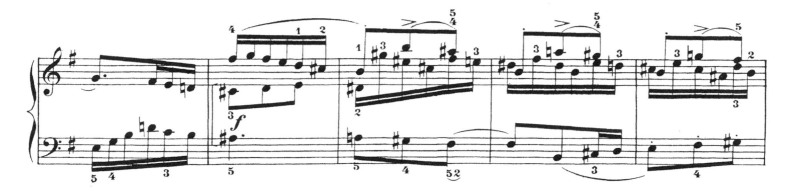

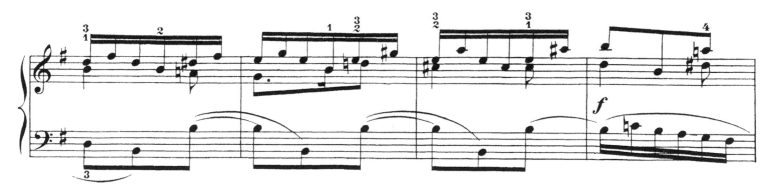

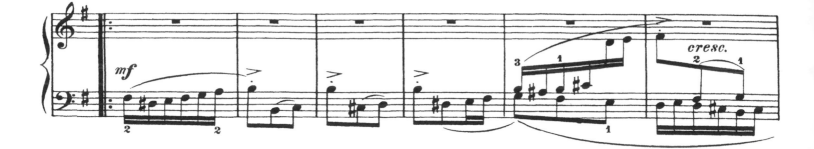

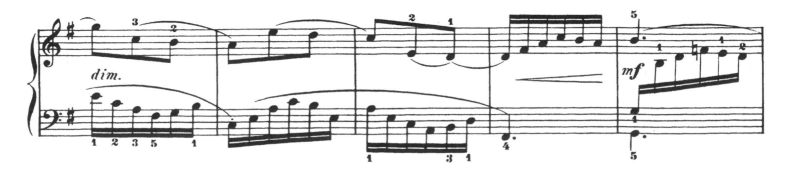

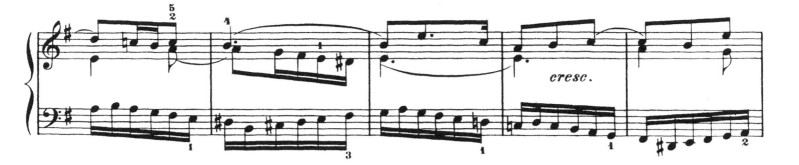

Courante
from French Suite No. 2 in C minor

Johann Sebastian Bach
BWV 813

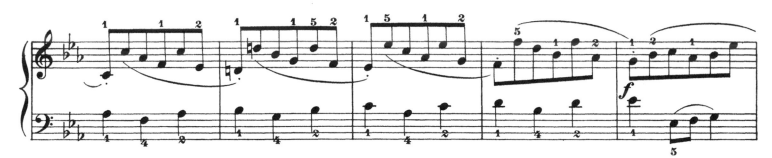

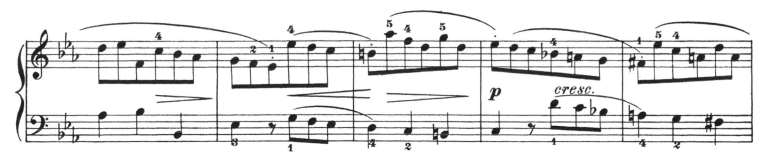

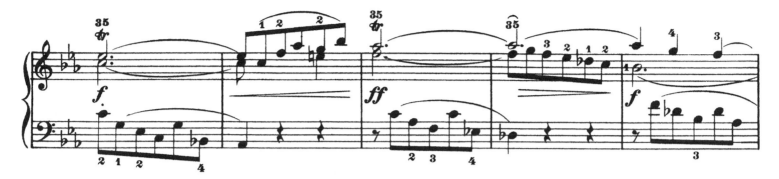

Allemande
from French Suite No. 3 in B minor

Johann Sebastian Bach
BWV 814

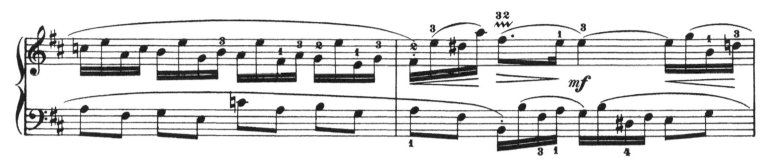

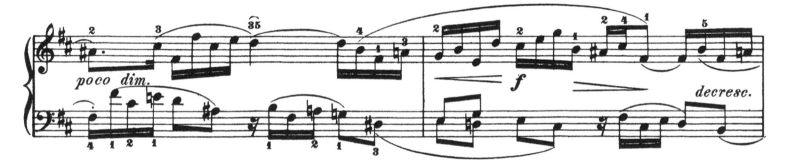

Gavotte and Bourée
from French Suite No. 5 in G Major

Johann Sebastian Bach
BWV 816

Un poco vivace (♩ = 88) Gavotte

Allegro (♩ = 96) Bourrée

Prelude
from Partita No. 1 in B-flat Major

Johann Sebastian Bach
BWV 825

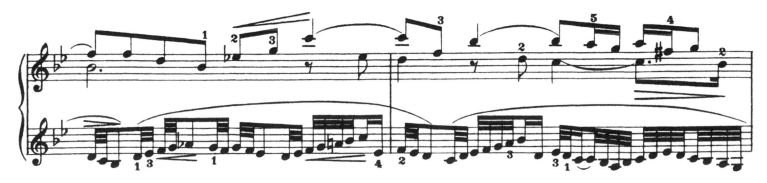

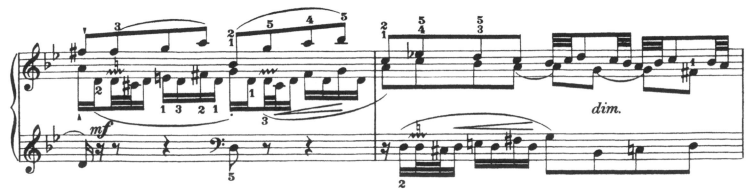

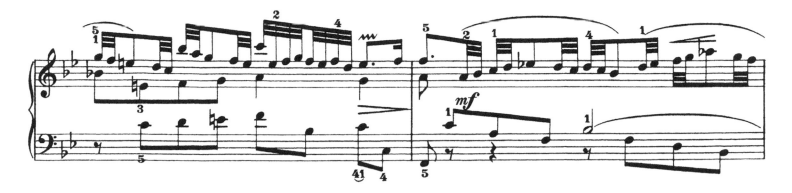

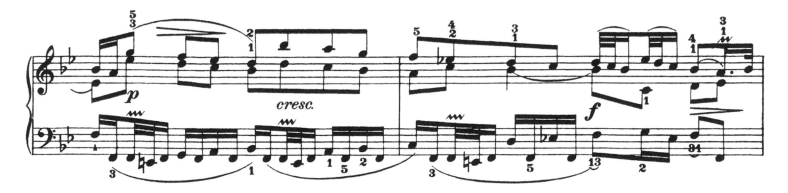

Sarabande
from Partita No. 2 in C minor

Johann Sebastian Bach
BWV 826

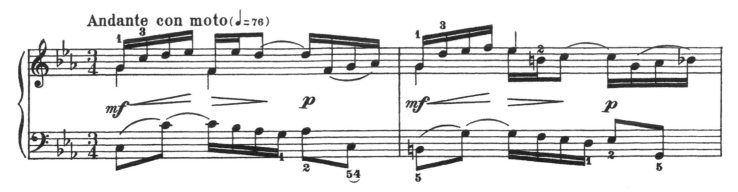

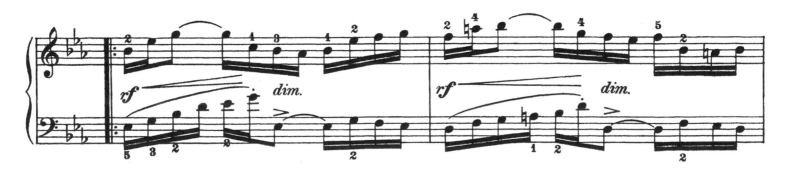

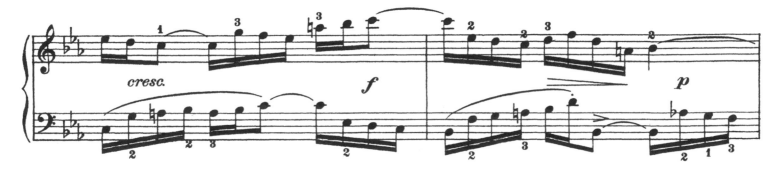

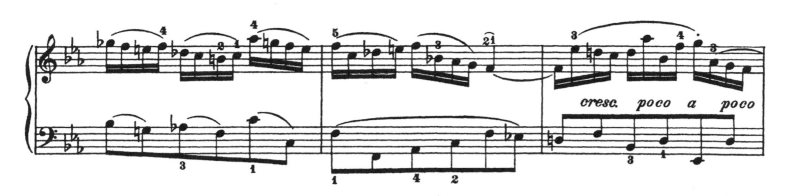

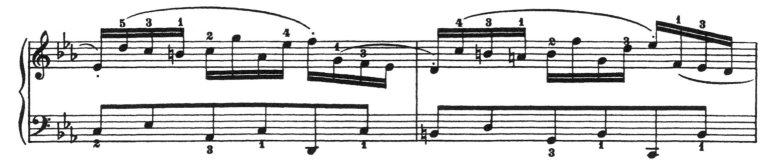

Rondeau
from Partita No. 2 in C minor

Johann Sebastian Bach
BWV 826

Prelude and Fugue No. 1 in C Major

from *The Well-Tempered Clavier*, Book 1

Johann Sebastian Bach
BWV 846

Prelude

All figures in the fingering which are set above the notes are intended, whether in inner or outer parts, for the right rand; whereas, the figures below the notes are for the left hand. This explanation will suffice to show, in doubtful cases, by which hand any note in the parts is to be played.

Fugue

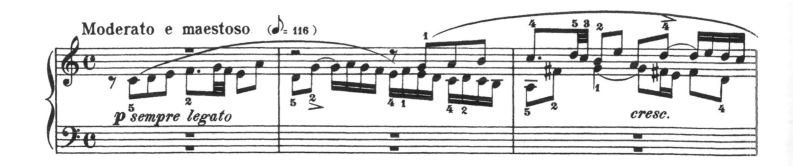

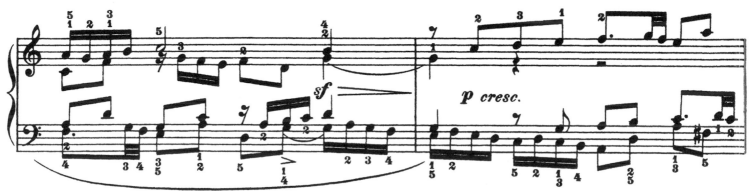

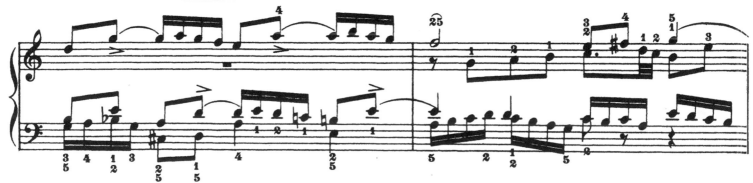

Prelude and Fugue No. 2 in C minor

from *The Well-Tempered Clavier*, Book 1

Johann Sebastian Bach

BWV 847

Prelude

Allegro vivace (♩ = 144)

Fugue

Allegretto moderato ($\quarternote$ = 80)

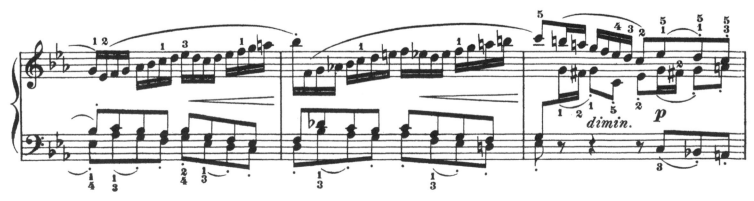

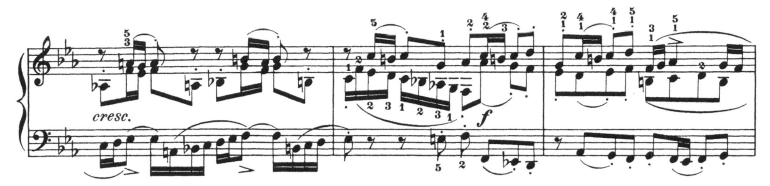

Prelude and Fugue No. 3 in C-sharp Major

from *The Well-Tempered Clavier*, Book 1

Prelude

Johann Sebastian Bach

BWV 848

Fugue

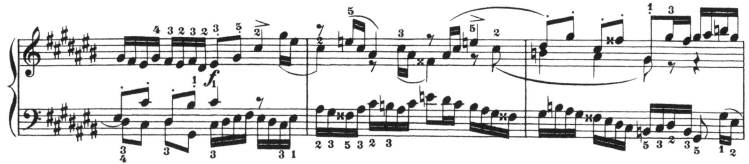

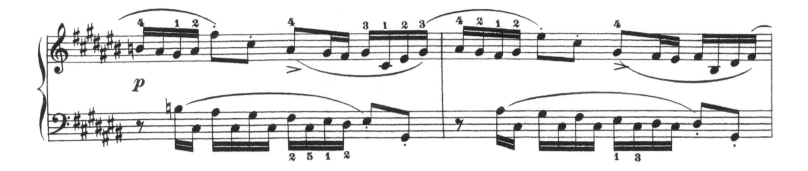

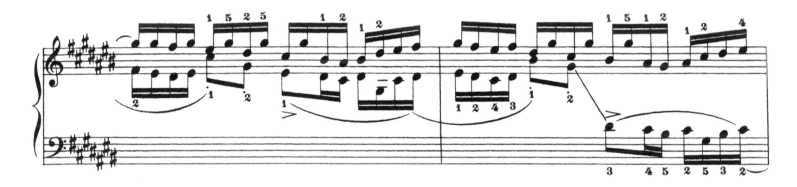

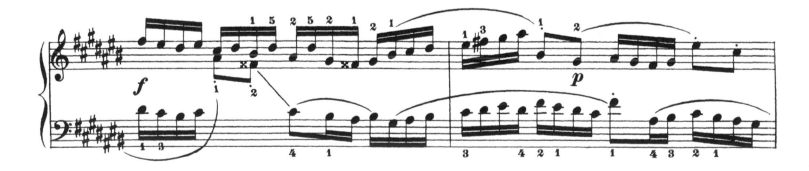

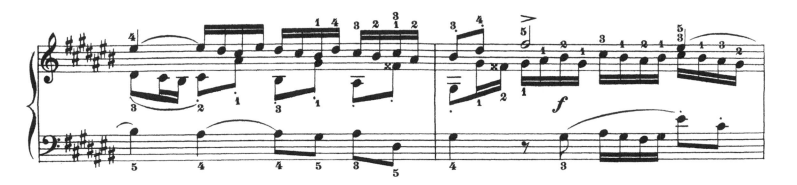

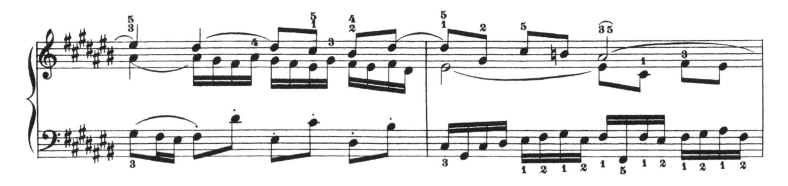

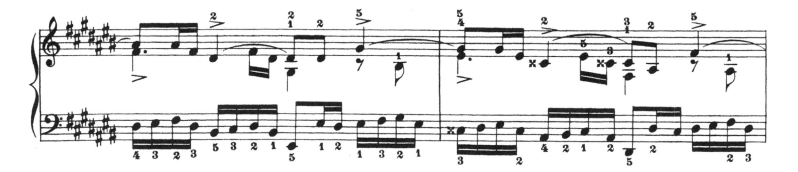

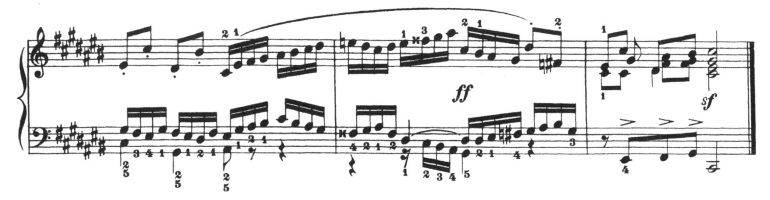

Prelude and Fugue No. 17 in A-flat Major

from *The Well-Tempered Clavier, Book 1*

Johann Sebastian Bach

BWV 862

Prelude

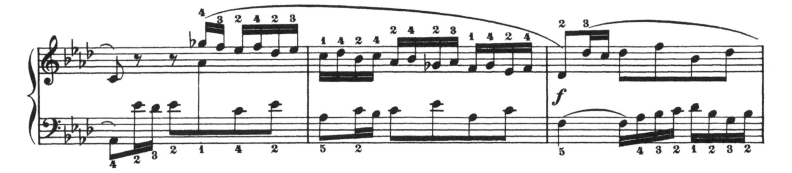

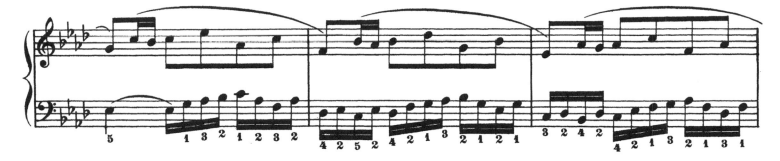

Fugue

Prelude and Fugue No. 21 in B-flat Major

from *The Well-Tempered Clavier*, Book 1

Johann Sebastian Bach

BWV 866

Prelude

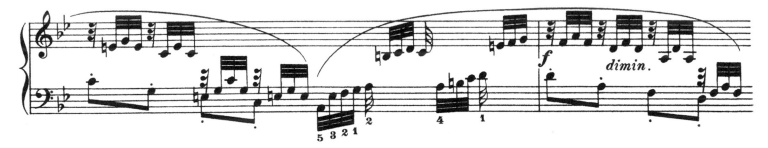

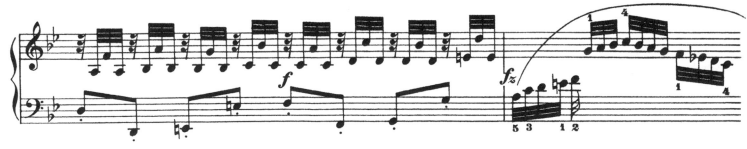

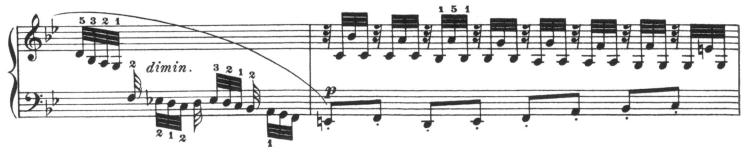

50

Fugue

Allegro vivace (♩ = 116)

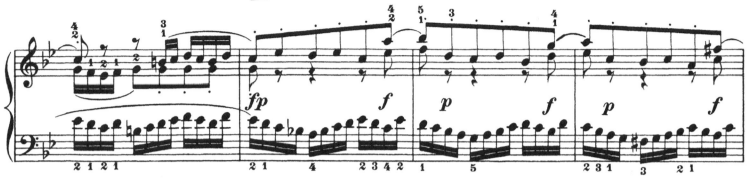

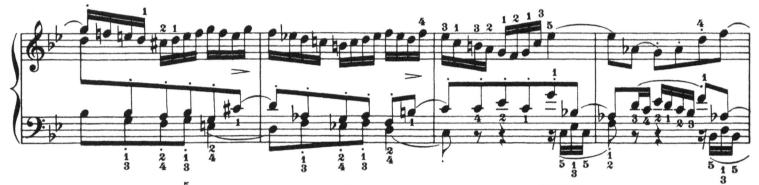

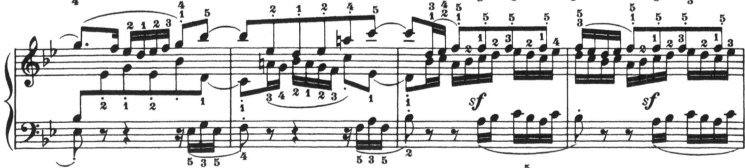

Prelude in C Major

Johann Sebastian Bach
BWV 924

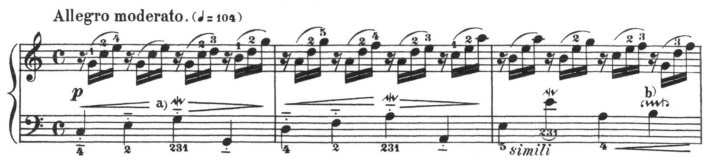

Prelude in D minor

Johann Sebastian Bach

BWV 926

Moderato tranquillo

Prelude in C minor

Johann Sebastian Bach
BWV 999

Prelude in C Major

Johann Sebastian Bach
BWV 939

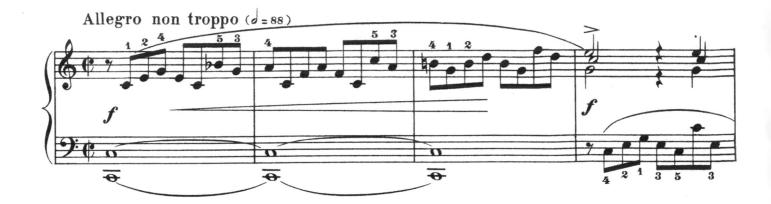

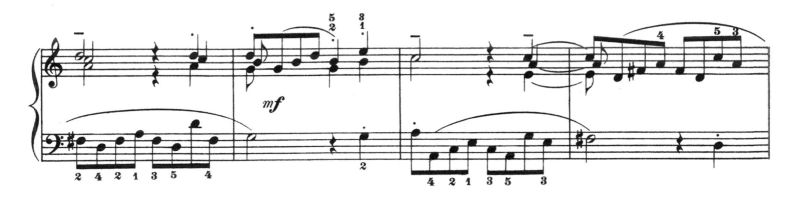